W9-CNO-281

See Them Grow

FROG

by Anastasiya Vasilyeva

Consultant: Sara Viernum
Wildlife Biologist and Herpetologist
Cofounder of The Wandering Herpetologist

BEARPORT
PUBLISHING

New York, New York

597.8
VAS

Credits

Cover, © Design Pics Inc/Alamy; Title page, © JIANG HONGYAN/Shutterstock; TOC, © sjk2012/Shutterstock and © Robin Arnold/iStock; 4–5, © Jeff Goulden/iStock; 6, © Chris Hill/Shutterstock; 7, © rmarnold/iStock; 7B, © Pukhov Konstantin/Shutterstock; 8, © ER Degginger/Science Source; 9, © Cllhnstev/Dreamstime; 10, © Dan Suzio/Science Source; 11, © ER Degginger/Science Source; 12–13, © Dan Suzio/Science Source; 14, © Ryu Uchiyama/Nature Production/Minden Pictures; 15, © Modoki Masuda/Nature Production/Minden Pictures; 16, © Ryu Uchiyama/Nature Production/Minden Pictures; 17, © KARL H. SWITAK/Science Photo Library/Science Source; 18, © JIANG HONGYAN/Shutterstock; 19, © Treat Davidson/FLPA/Minden Pictures; 20, © WILDLIFE GmbH/Alamy; 21, © Dwight Kuhn; 22, © sjk2012/Shutterstock and © Ryan M. Bolton/Shutterstock; 23 (T to B), © moonoi172/Shutterstock, © Cllhnstev/Dreamstime, © purplequeue/Shutterstock, © JIANG HONGYAN/Shutterstock, and © JIANG HONGYAN/Shutterstock; 24, © feathercollector/Shutterstock.

Publisher: Kenn Goin
Senior Editor: Joyce Tavolacci
Creative Director: Spencer Brinker
Design: Debrah Kaiser
Photo Researcher: Thomas Persano

Library of Congress Cataloging-in-Publication Data

Names: Vasilyeva, Anastasiya, author.
Title: Frog / by Anastasiya Vasilyeva.
Description: New York, New York : Bearport Publishing, [2017] | Series: See them grow | Audience: Ages 5–8. | Includes bibliographical references and index.
Identifiers: LCCN 2016038812 (print) | LCCN 2016045159 (ebook) | ISBN 9781684020409 (library) | ISBN 9781684020928 (ebook)
Subjects: LCSH: Bullfrog—Life cycles—Juvenile literature. | CYAC: Frogs—Life cycles.
Classification: LCC QL668.E27 V37 2017 (print) | LCC QL668.E27 (ebook) | DDC 597.8/92—dc23
LC record available at https://lccn.loc.gov/2016038812

For more information, write to Bearport Publishing Company, Inc., 45 West 21st Street, Suite 3B, New York, New York 10010. Printed in the United States of America.

10 9 8 7 6 5 4 3 2 1

Contents

Frog

Splash! A bullfrog hops into a pond.

The animal is big and green.

It has webbed feet and moist skin.

How did it get that way?

Bullfrogs are the biggest frogs in North America.

5

It's springtime.

Grr-rum! Grr-rum!

A male bullfrog calls to a female.

male
bullfrog

It's time to **mate.**

female
bullfrog

A bullfrog's deep, loud call sounds like a bull roaring. That's how the animal got its name.

After mating, the female frog lays a huge clump of eggs in the pond.

Each tiny egg looks like a ball of clear jelly.

A female bullfrog can lay up to 20,000 eggs at one time!

In the middle of the egg is a small black dot.

This is the **embryo.**

Over time, it will grow into a bullfrog!

After only about a day, the embryo grows a tiny tail bud.

Then it begins to form a mouth.

It starts to look like a small fish.

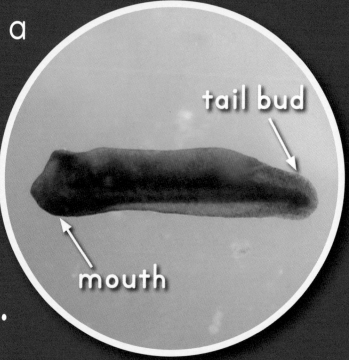

tail bud

mouth

Inside its mouth, the embryo grows rows of little teeth.

The embryo grows larger.

When it's three to five days old, it hatches!

tail

A small black **tadpole** wiggles out of the egg.

It uses its tail to swim through the water.

The tadpole breathes with **gills**— just like a fish!

The tadpole feeds on **algae** and water plants.

It eats a lot and gets bigger and bigger.

It can take a few months or up to three years for the tadpole to grow tiny back legs.

back leg

During this time, the tadpole still lives in the water.

If a tadpole is attacked and loses its tail, it can grow a new one!

After several more months, the tadpole grows front legs.

Now it's known as a froglet.

Yet it still has a tail.

In cold areas, a tadpole can take several years to grow into a bullfrog.

The froglet loses its gills and breathes with lungs.

Now it can live on land!

The froglet grows and grows.

Finally, its tail disappears.

It's now an adult bullfrog!

webbed
feet

A bullfrog's webbed feet and strong back legs make it a good swimmer.

The adult bullfrog will eat anything that fits into its big mouth.

This little animal can grow to be 8 inches (20 cm) long!

fish

worm

A bullfrog can live for up to ten years in the wild.

Frog Facts

- As bullfrogs grow, they shed their old skin. Then they eat it!

- Bullfrogs use their big eyes to help them swallow food. When eating, they close their eyes and push them against the back of their mouths. This helps move food down their throats!

- Bullfrogs often rest during the day and hunt for food at night.

- Did you know that bullfrogs help humans? They eat annoying bugs, like mosquitoes.

Glossary

 **algae** (AL-jee) tiny plantlike living things that grow in water

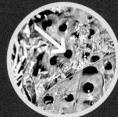 **embryo** (EM-bree-oh) an animal in the first stage of development

 **gills** (GILZ) body parts used by fish and other water animals to breathe

 **mate** (MAYT) to come together to have young

 **tadpole** (TAD-pohl) the immature form of a frog

Index

Read More

Rice, Dona Herweck. *A Frog's Life.* Huntington Beach, CA: Teacher Created Materials (2011).

Wallace, Karen. *Tale of a Tadpole.* New York: DK (2015).

Zoehfeld, Kathleen Weidner. *From Tadpole to Frog.* New York: Scholastic (2011).

Learn More Online

To learn more about frogs, visit
www.bearportpublishing.com/SeeThemGrow

About the Author

Anastasiya Vasilyeva lives in New York City. As a kid, she loved to play with slippery tadpoles.